# Grandmother's
## SCRAPBOOK OF MEMORIES™

**Made especially for**

_____

FROM

_____

DATE

Surprisingly Simple
*A LASTING
GIFT of LOVE*

PLACE YOUR PHOTO HERE

INTEGRITY®
PUBLISHERS
*Nashville*

# I Love Being Your Grandmother!

# Before I Was a Grandmother

# Grandmother's Blessings, Dreams, and Advice

# How to Create Your Scrapbook of Memories™

**CONGRATULATIONS!** You have found the perfect gift for your grandchild! Just add memories, and you have a one-of-a-kind keepsake that will be treasured for a lifetime.

As you browse the pages of this scrapbook, think back over precious memories and unforgettable moments. As you fill each page with your thoughts, prayers, and remembrances, you are creating a customized token of love that can be shared with generations to come.

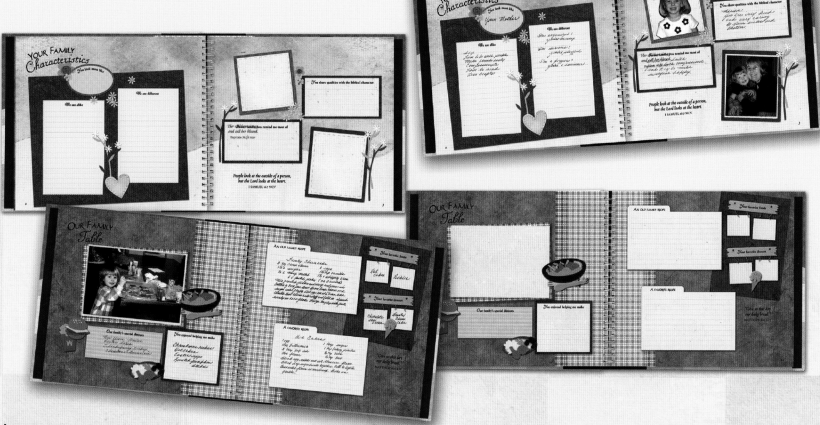

## It's easy!

1. Look back over the special times you've had with your grandchild, and record your memories with the help of the prompts provided on each page. (Unsure of some of the details? No problem! Save those prompts as a special opportunity to finish creating the scrapbook with the help of your grandchild.)
2. Gather favorite photographs and place them in the spaces provided.
3. Write a personal letter to your grandchild in the space provided.
4. Tear out this page.
5. Save this Scrapbook of Memories for that special occasion, and then giggle, cry, and dream along with your grandchild as you recall all of the memories you've shared together.

### THEY'LL NEVER FORGET THE GIFT OF A SCRAPBOOK OF MEMORIES!

**Scrapbook of Memories™ Series**

*Grandmother's* SCRAPBOOK OF MEMORIES

*Mom's* SCRAPBOOK OF MEMORIES

*Sisters* *scrapbook of memories*

**Friends** Scrapbook of Memories

GRADUATE'S *Scrapbook of Memories*

# A Letter to My Grandchild

*I thank my God upon every remembrance of you.*

PHILIPPIANS 1:3 NKJV

# The Day I Became Your Grandmother

When I learned I was going to be your grandmother

_____
_____
_____
_____
_____
_____

NAME

BORN ON

AT

WEIGHT          LENGTH

PARENTS

PLACE

*The* first time I saw you

_____
_____
_____
_____
_____
_____
_____
_____
_____
_____
_____
_____
_____
_____

*Children are a gift from the* LORD.

PSALM 127: 3 NLT

# YOUR Parents

YOUR MOTHER

DATE OF BIRTH

*How* you are like your mom

*Wh*at I love most about your mom

*W*hat I love most about your dad

_____
_____
_____
_____
_____
_____
_____
_____
_____
_____
_____
_____
_____
_____
_____
_____
_____
_____
_____

YOUR FATHER

DATE OF BIRTH

*H*ow you are like your dad

_____
_____

*May your father and mother be glad;*
*may she who gave you birth rejoice!*

PROVERBS 23:25 NIV

9

# YOUR FAMILY
## Characteristics

You look most like

We are different

We are alike

You share qualities with the biblical character

_____

_____

_____

_____

In our family, you remind me most of

_____

_____

_____

_____

_____

_____

*"People look at the outside of a person,
but the Lord looks at the heart."*

I Samuel 16:7 ncv

# Your Moments of Wonder

Where you found happiness

Some of the cutest things you said

The funny things you did

"Stand still and consider the wondrous works of God."

JOB 37:14 NKJV

I enjoyed watching you

You couldn't wait to grow up and be

# YOUR CHILDHOOD Favorites

Your favorite

Food

Game

Song

CHOCOLATE

Baby Bear Story

Book

Movie

Bedtime prayer

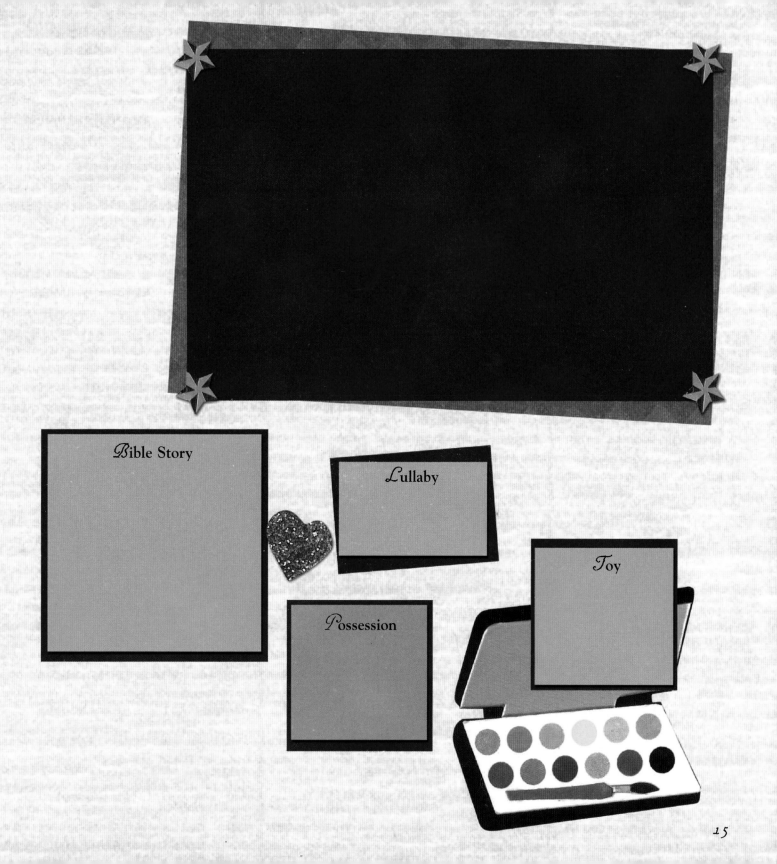

Bible Story

Lullaby

Possession

Toy

# Our Family Life

On birthdays, we celebrate

Our family is important to me because

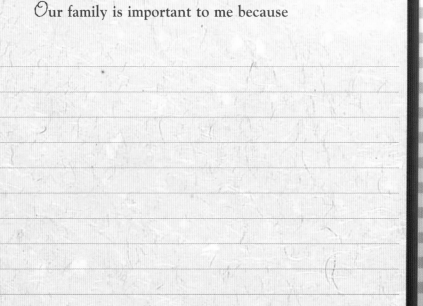

Train up a child in the way he
should go, and when he is old
he will not depart from it.

PROVERBS 22:6 NKJV

Some of our family goals

The activities we enjoy together

We make time for God by

# OUR FAMILY Faith

Our family is blessed by

_____

_____

_____

_____

_____

_____

_____

_____

_____

_____

_____

_____

_____

Our family believes

_____

_____

$\mathcal{M}$y prayer for our family

_____
_____
_____
_____
_____
_____
_____
_____
_____
_____
_____
_____
_____
_____
_____
_____

$\mathcal{F}$avorite family scriptures

_____
_____
_____
_____
_____
_____
_____

"But as for me and my
household, we will serve
the LORD."

JOSHUA 24:15 NIV

# OUR FAMILY *Table*

Our family's special dinners

You enjoyed helping me make

AN OLD FAMILY RECIPE

Your favorite dessert

A FAVORITE RECIPE

"Give us this day
our daily bread."
MATTHEW 6:11 KJV

# Our Family Vacations

Your favorite family vacation

*"The LORD your God is with you wherever you go."*

JOSHUA 1:9 NLT

A memorable trip we took together

_____
_____
_____
_____
_____
_____
_____
_____
_____
_____
_____
_____

Special visits with family members

_____
_____
_____
_____
_____
_____
_____
_____
_____
_____
_____
_____

Your favorite cousin

# Our Christmas Traditions

In our family, Christmas means

At Christmas, we

Our family Christmas traditions

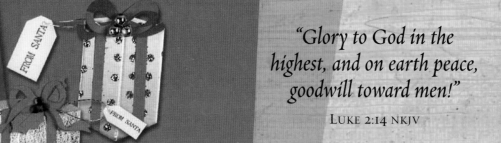

*"Glory to God in the highest, and on earth peace, goodwill toward men!"*

LUKE 2:14 NKJV

A SPECIAL CHRISTMAS RECIPE

A SPECIAL CHRISTMAS RECIPE

25

# GROWING WITH God

You were baptized/dedicated

_____
DATE

_____
PLACE

*Be strong in the faith, just as you were taught, and always be thankful.*

Colossians 2:7 NCV

The church you attended as a child

You learned about God by

Favorite church songs

I pray God uses you to

# Our Relationship

**What I admire most about you**

_____
_____
_____
_____
_____
_____
_____
_____
_____
_____
_____
_____
_____
_____
_____
_____
_____
_____
_____
_____
_____
_____
_____
_____

**You have positively influenced my life**

_____
_____
_____
_____
_____
_____

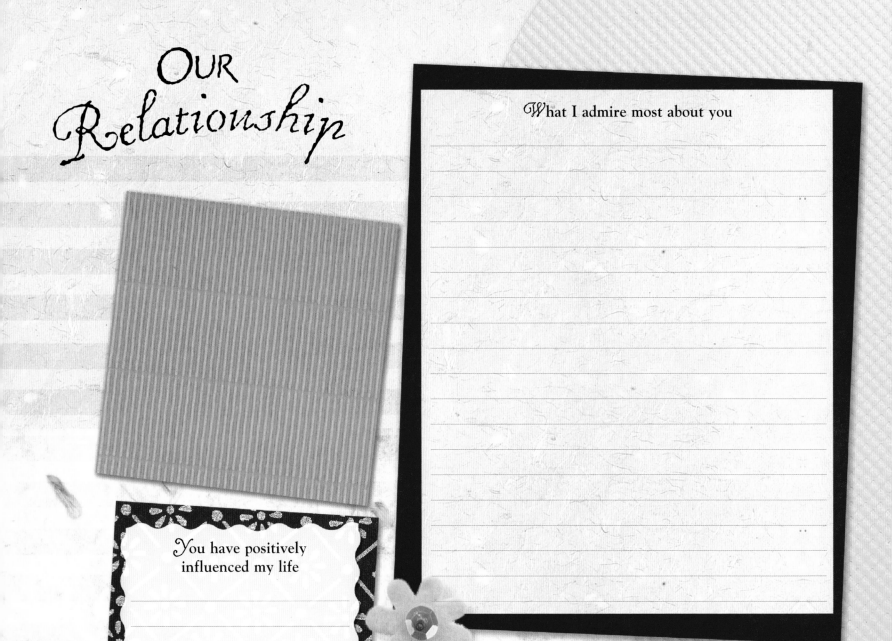

I love you because

"Just as the Father has loved Me, I have also loved you; abide in My love."

JOHN 15:9 NASB

We are similar in that

We are different in that

# OUR TIMES
## Together

**When you and I are alone**

Apple Crumb

Banana Nut

Blueberry

Favorite games to play

My nickname(s) for you

Classic Games
Checkers

Enjoy this classic game with
friends and family!

AGES
8 UP

Favorite songs to sing

I enjoyed talking with you about

Can two walk together,
except they be agreed?

AMOS 3:3 KJV

31

# WHEN I WAS Born

NAME

_____

BORN ON

_____

AT

_____

PLACE

_____

PARENTS

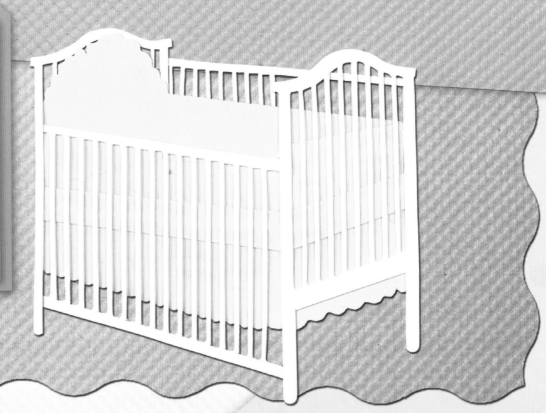

*I will praise You, for I am fearfully and wonderfully made; marvelous are Your works, and that my soul knows very well.*

Psalm 139:14 NKJV

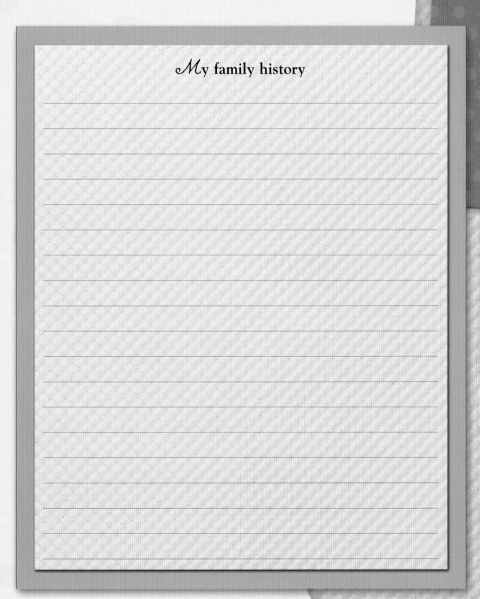

My family history

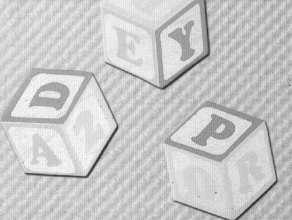

My name was chosen

# My Childhood World

## Some things that have improved

## The president when I was born

## News headlines when I was born

## Social issues

$\mathcal{M}$y childhood world was different from yours in that

_____

_____

_____

_____

_____

_____

_____

_____

_____

_____

_____

_____

_____

_____

THE COST OF THINGS

ITEM

PRICE

ITEM

PRICE

ITEM

PRICE

$\mathcal{M}$y family car

*Trust in Him at all times.*

PSALM 62:8 NKJV

# My Mother
## (Your Great-Grandmother)

MAIDEN NAME

BIRTH DATE

BIRTH PLACE

The best advice she gave me

The sweetest memory of my mother

Cherry Pie

*Her children rise up*
*and call her blessed.*

PROVERBS 31:28 NKJV

*W*hat I admire most about my mother

_____
_____
_____
_____
_____
_____
_____
_____

*F*rom my mother, I learned that God

_____
_____
_____
_____
_____
_____
_____
_____

*M*y mother shared qualities with the biblical character

# My Father

## (Your Great-Grandfather)

The dearest memory of him

_____
_____
_____
_____
_____
_____
_____
_____
_____
_____
_____
_____
_____
_____
_____
_____
_____
_____
_____

My father shared qualities with
the biblical character

_____
NAME

_____
BIRTH DATE

_____
BIRTH PLACE

From my father,
I learned that God

_"Honor your father
and your mother."_

EXODUS 20:12 NASB

The best advice he gave me

# ABOUT
## My Family

_____

AND

_____

WERE UNITED IN HOLY MATRIMONY ON

_____

DATE

_____

LOCATION

My siblings' names and birth dates

_____

_____

_____

_____

_____

_____

_____

_____

My personality was most like

_____

_____

_____

_____

_____

In my family, I look most like

# WHEN I WAS A CHILD

My favorite childhood experience

My childhood home

The toughest part of growing up

_____
_____
_____
_____
_____
_____
_____
_____
_____
_____

*Be happy...while you
are young, and let your
heart give you joy in the
days of your youth.*

ECCLESIASTES 11:9 NIV

Things I enjoyed

_____
_____
_____
_____
_____

I always wanted to be

_____
_____
_____
_____
_____
_____
_____

# When I Was A Teenager

"Dating" in my generation

_____
_____
_____
_____
_____
_____
_____
_____
_____
_____
_____
_____
_____
_____
_____

My first car was

_____
NAME

_____
DATE

_____
MAKE

_____
MODEL

_____
YEAR

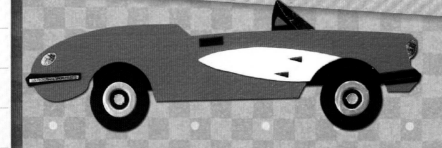

# Popular fashion trends

_____
_____
_____
_____
_____
_____
_____
_____
_____
_____
_____
_____

My first job

Year when I first voted in an election

# My Education

School(s) I attended

Favorite Subject(s)

Least Favorite Subject(s)

Graduation Year(s)

*W*hat I dreamed of doing
when I grew up

_____

_____

_____

_____

_____

*A*ctivities and social groups

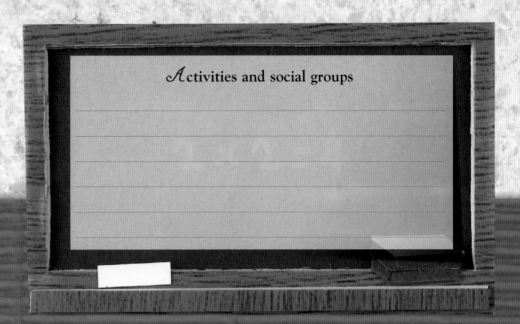

*A* memorable school experience

_____

_____

_____

_____

_____

_____

_____

_____

_____

_____

_____

MATH

ENGLISH

*The wise person makes*
*learning a joy.*

PROVERBS 15:2 NLT

# My Family Times

*Your family will be a blessing to all people.*

GENESIS 28:14 CEV

*G*od blessed my family by

*M*y family spent time together

*I*n my family, we held strong beliefs in

Family reunions we've had over the years

The things we do
together today

# My Travels

*"The LORD your God will be with you wherever you go."*

JOSHUA 1:9 NIV

*M*y family vacations

*M*y first plane ride

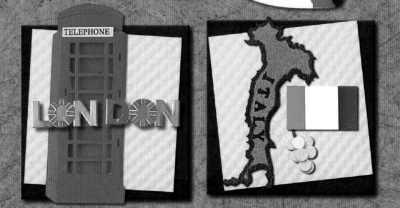

My favorite trip

Someday I'd like to see

MEXICO

# My Holiday Traditions

My favorite holiday
_____
_____
_____
_____
_____
_____
_____

How we celebrated Easter
_____
_____
_____
_____
_____

How we celebrated Independence Day
_____
_____
_____

How we celebrated Thanksgiving
_____
_____
_____
_____
_____

A THANKSGIVING RECIPE

_____
_____
_____
_____
_____
_____
_____
_____
_____
_____

*Celebrate these days with feasting and gladness and by giving gifts to each other and to the poor.*

ESTHER 9:22 NLT

A NEW YEAR'S RECIPE

_____
_____
_____
_____
_____
_____
_____
_____

# My Faith

I was baptized/dedicated

_____
DATE

_____
PLACE

*I* feel God's direction in my life

_____
_____
_____
_____
_____
_____
_____
_____
_____
_____

$\mathcal{A}$ turning point in my faith

"*The righteous will live by faith.*"

ROMANS 1:17 NIV

The church I attended as a child

# In My Garden

Fig

grass

I now enjoy growing

_____
_____
_____
_____
_____

𝒜s a child, we grew

_____
_____
_____
_____
_____
_____
_____
_____
_____
_____
_____
_____
_____
_____
_____
_____

56

"I am the true vine,
and my Father is the gardener."

JOHN 15:1 NLT

Gardening hints

My favorite flower

# Inspirations

### Greatest spiritual influences

_____
_____
_____
_____
_____
_____
_____
_____
_____
_____
_____
_____
_____
_____
_____

### The qualities I admire in a person

_____
_____
_____
_____
_____
_____
_____

### My role models/personal heroes

_____
_____
_____
_____
_____
_____
_____

_Whoever walks with the wise
will become wise._

PROVERBS 13:20 NLT

# The most influential people in my life

_____

_____

_____

_____

_____

_____

_____

_____

_____

_____

_____

_____

_____

_____

_____

_____

# FEATS AND Defeats

The most difficult thing about being an adult

The greatest life lessons that I've learned

My greatest accomplishments

_____
_____
_____
_____
_____
_____
_____
_____
_____
_____
_____

*Those who trust in the LORD…will not be defeated*
*but will endure forever.*

PSALM 125:1 NLT

Some of my future goals

_____
_____
_____
_____
_____
_____
_____
_____
_____

A successful life is

_____
_____
_____
_____
_____
_____

# My Favorite Things

Food

Color

Movie

Song

TV show

Scripture

Cherry Pie

Actor/Actress

Way to spend a rainy day

Season

Time of day

Possession

Jewelry

# MY CUP of Tea

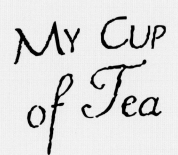

**My hobbies**

**Where I like to spend my spare time**

**Religious groups I am active in**

*God has made everything beautiful for its own time.*

ECCLESIASTES 3:11 NLT

Something I would like
to do with you

# My Love Story

He caught my eye because

When I met your grandfather

Love

## Our courtship

_____
_____
_____
_____
_____
_____
_____
_____
_____
_____
_____
_____
_____
_____
_____
_____
_____

## What I admire most about your grandfather

_____
_____
_____
_____
_____
_____

## How your grandfather proposed

_____
_____
_____
_____
_____
_____
_____
_____
_____

*Many waters cannot
quench love; rivers cannot
wash it away.*

SONG OF SONGS 8:7 NIV

# My Wedding

_____

AND

_____

WERE UNITED IN
HOLY MATRIMONY ON

_____

DATE

_____

LOCATION

*Let us love one another.*

1 JOHN 4:7 NIV

*G*od teaches us that love

_____
_____
_____
_____
_____

*A* prosperous marriage

_____
_____
_____
_____
_____
_____
_____
_____
_____
_____
_____
_____

*T*he most difficult part
of marriage

_____
_____
_____
_____
_____
_____
_____
_____
_____
_____
_____
_____

*M*y role as a wife

_____
_____
_____
_____
_____
_____
_____
_____
_____
_____
_____
_____

# My OWN Family

To me, family is

As a family, we believe

Our children's names and birth dates

"I will take care of you."

JEREMIAH 1:19 NLT

Activities we did as a family

BEING A
Grandmother

The best part of being your grandmother

The love of a grandmother

*I* hope that I've taught my children and grandchildren

_____

_____

_____

_____

_____

_____

_____

_____

_____

_____

_____

_____

*You should be known for the beauty that comes from within, the unfading beauty of a gentle and quiet spirit, which is so precious to God.*

1 PETER 3:4 NLT

*W*hen you are a grandparent, take time to

_____

_____

_____

_____

_____

_____

# LIVING AND *Learning*

A life lesson I'm glad I learned

_____
_____
_____
_____
_____
_____
_____
_____
_____

The principles that guide me

_____
_____
_____
_____
_____
_____
_____

*"Wisdom belongs to the aged, and understanding to those who have lived many years."*

JOB 12:12 NLT

Something I wish I had known
when I was younger

_____
_____
_____
_____
_____
_____

Something I wish I had done

_____
_____
_____
_____
_____
_____
_____

What I value most in life

_____
_____
_____
_____
_____
_____
_____
_____
_____
_____
_____
_____
_____
_____
_____
_____
_____
_____
_____
_____
_____
_____
_____
_____
_____

# FOR YOUR *Future*

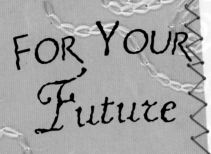

**M**y blessing for you

"Be strong and do not give up,
for your work will be rewarded."

2 CHRONICLES 15:7 NIV

The best advice I've been given

My advice to you on love

My advice to you on faith

My advice to you on growing older

# MY PRAYERS for You

*I pray that your marriage*

*My prayer for you*

My prayer for your children

I will always love you because

LOVE

I Love You

A special Bible verse for you

I hope you have learned that God

JOLEE'S BOUTIQUE® STICKERS AND JOLEE'S BY YOU™ EMBELLISHMENTS ARE OFFERED IN HUNDREDS OF INTRICATE STYLES DESIGNED FOR SCRAPBOOKING, CARD MAKING, AND PAPER CRAFTS. EACH WELL-CRAFTED DIMENSIONAL ACCENT IS MADE FROM A MIX OF MATERIALS—FROM PAPERS, WOOD, FIBERS, FABRICS, METALS, FOILS, AND BOTANICALS. THEY ARE SOLD AT SCRAPBOOK, CRAFT, AND STATIONERY STORES THROUGHOUT THE COUNTRY.